AmericanGirl Library™

Crafts
for Girls

This book is dedicated to my mother, Nancy Ballou
Williams, the best teacher I have known. She taught me
in art, as in life, there is no such thing as failure.
Sally Seamans

Published by Pleasant Company Publications
© Copyright 1995 by Pleasant Company

First Edition.
Printed in the United States of America.
95 96 97 98 99 WCR 10 9 8 7 6 5 4 3 2 1

American Girl Library™ is a trademark of Pleasant Company.

Editorial Development by Jeanette Wall
Art Direction: Kym Abrams
Design: Gail Rogoznica-McKernin
Tabletop Photography: Mike Walker
Model Photography: Paul Tryba

Portions of this book have previously been published in
American Girl® magazine.

Photo Credits: Pages 1 and 29: Arthur Tilley/FPG International
Pages 2 and 45: Jade Albert/FPG International
Page 29: Frank Siteman/The Picture Cube

Library of Congress Cataloging-in-Publication Data
Seamans, Sally.
Crafts for girls / by Sally Seamans ; illustrated by Judy Pelikan.
—1st ed.
p. cm. — (American girl)
ISBN 1-56247-229-1
1. Handicraft—Juvenile literature. [1. Handicraft.]
I. Pelikan, Judy, ill. II. Title.
TT171.S43 1995 745.5—dc20 95-6743 CIP AC

★AmericanGirl Library™

Crafts
for Girls

By Sally Seamans
Illustrated by Judy Pelikan

PLEASANT
COMPANY
PUBLICATIONS™

Contents

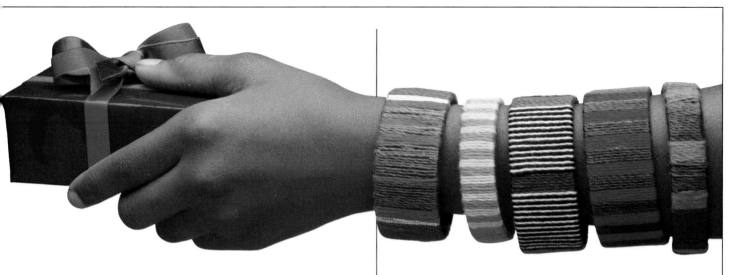

Getting Started

Take some ordinary materials, a little time, and your own imagination, and get an original work of art to keep or a one-of-a-kind gift to be treasured!

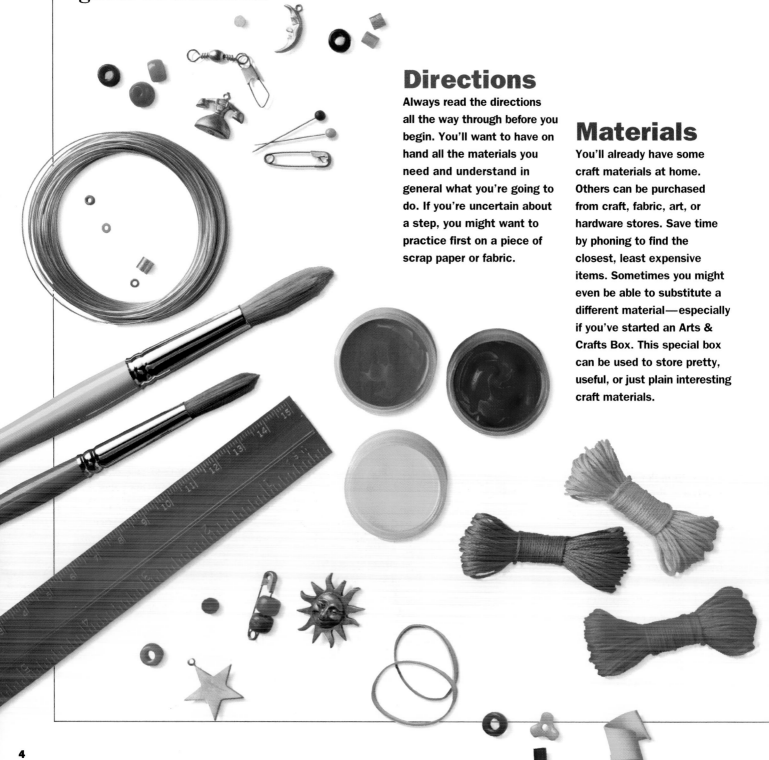

Directions

Always read the directions all the way through before you begin. You'll want to have on hand all the materials you need and understand in general what you're going to do. If you're uncertain about a step, you might want to practice first on a piece of scrap paper or fabric.

Materials

You'll already have some craft materials at home. Others can be purchased from craft, fabric, art, or hardware stores. Save time by phoning to find the closest, least expensive items. Sometimes you might even be able to substitute a different material—especially if you've started an Arts & Crafts Box. This special box can be used to store pretty, useful, or just plain interesting craft materials.

Very Important!

This hand and heart symbol means you'll need special help from an adult, usually for safety reasons. Of course, *always* follow your family safety rules when using cutting tools, the stove, or the oven. Carefully read the labels and warnings for materials like glues, paints, and acrylic sprays.

Time

The approximate amount of time to make each craft is noted in the "You Will Need" list. This time does not include baking and drying time. Sometimes the drying time for glue or paint or papier-mâché is much longer than the time needed to actually make the craft. To be sure that you have enough time to complete a craft in one sitting, read all the steps.

Work Area

Pick a well-lighted place that's out of reach of pets and younger children. Be sure to protect your work surface, using wax paper, an old plastic tablecloth, or newspapers. Protect your clothes by wearing an apron or smock. Finally, remember to clean up afterwards, putting all your supplies back where they belong.

Crown of Flowers

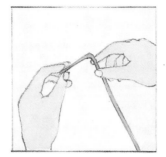

1 Attach the two floral wires to each other so they will be long enough to go around your head. To do this, first bend in about 1 inch of wire at one end of each wire.

2 Attach these two "hooks" of wire to each other as shown. Squeeze the hooks so they are tightly joined.

3 Wrap the wire around your head to measure how long it should be. Have an adult help you cut off what you don't need with wire cutters, leaving an extra inch or so of wire on each end. Bend over 1 inch of wire to make a hook at one end.

With blossoms and buds and leaves of green, weave
a wreath that's fit for a summer queen.

4 Cut a strip of floral tape 12 inches long. Wrap the strip around one end of the wire. Floral tape is slightly sticky so it will stay in place. As you wrap, fasten a flower to the wire by winding the tape around the stem a few times.

5 Keep cutting strips of tape and adding flowers all along the wire in the same way. You may find that the flowers look best facing in the same direction.

6 Wrap the crown around your head again and make a hook on the second end to fit your head. Hook the two ends together and squeeze so that the hooks tighten. Wrap a flower over the hooks with floral tape to hide them.

Use several flowers of different colors or just your favorite flower— daisies or violets or sunflowers, for example.

Napkin Rings

Turn plain wooden rings into bright, colorful napkin holders with ribbon and two-sided tape.

YOU WILL NEED

Time
- 15-30 minutes per ring

Supplies
- Two-sided tape with peel-off backing
- Wooden napkin rings
- Scissors
- Satin-like ribbon, ¼ inch wide—about 4 yards per napkin ring
- Ruler
- Glue stick or white glue

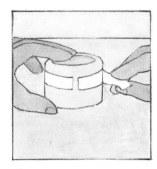

1 Wrap a piece of two-sided tape around the top half of a wooden napkin ring. Peel off the backing.

2 Wrap another piece of tape around the bottom half of the ring. Peel off the backing.

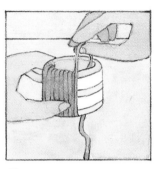

3 Cut a piece of ribbon about 2 yards long. Press the ribbon onto the tape and begin wrapping the ribbon around the ring. Slightly overlap each round of ribbon.

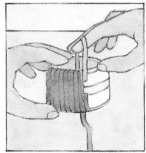

4 If you want to change to a different color, cut the ribbon, leaving about ¼ inch to press onto the tape. Then press about ¼ inch of the new color ribbon onto the tape.

5 Continue wrapping the ribbon around the ring. Wrap right over the cut ends of ribbon to hide them.

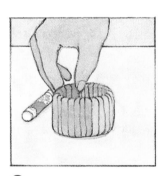

6 When the napkin ring is completely covered, cut the ribbon, leaving about a ¾-inch piece. Put glue on the inside of this piece and fold it inside the napkin ring. Press it in place until it stays by itself.

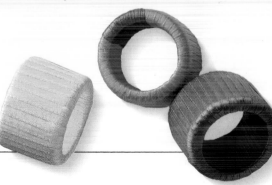

Papier-Mâché Bowl

1 In the plastic container, mix 4 level tablespoons of wallpaper paste with 4 cups of cold water. Stir this mixture well. Let it sit for at least 15 minutes. Then stir it again.

2 Cover your work surface with the plastic tablecloth. Tear the newspapers into strips about ¾ inch by 5 inches. (You will see that it's easy to tear newspaper straight in one direction but not in the other.)

3 Turn the bowl upside down on wax paper. Use a paper towel to rub a little petroleum jelly or salad oil on the outside of the bowl. Cover the outside of the bowl with plastic wrap.

Note: These bowls are for dry food only. Do not put them in the dishwasher. Clean with a damp sponge.

10

With newspaper and paste, make a project so pretty,
it will bowl everyone over!

 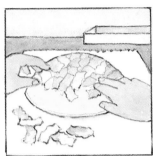 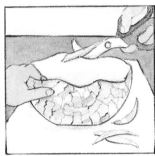 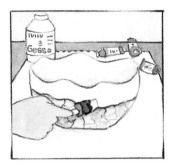

4 Dip a strip of newspaper into the wallpaper paste. Run the strip between two fingers to remove extra paste. The strip should be wet, but it should not have globs of paste on it. Lay the strip over the bottom of the bowl. Continue laying pasted strips on the bowl in an overlapping pattern until the bowl is totally covered.

5 Let the bowl dry completely on wax paper for a day or so. (Cover the wallpaper paste mixture and store it in a cupboard until you need it again.) Put at least five more coats of pasted newspaper strips on a large bowl and two or three more coats on a small bowl. Let each coat dry completely before starting the next.

6 Remove the papier-mâché bowl from the mold bowl. Gently remove the plastic wrap. With scissors, carefully cut the rim straight all the way around or make a wavy edge. Put one more layer of papier-mâché on the rim of the bowl and anywhere the bowl feels thin. Let it dry completely.

7 With the sponge brush, paint the bowl with gesso. Let it dry for 10 or 15 minutes and apply another coat. Let it dry. Then paint the bowl with acrylic paints and again let it dry. Have an adult spray the bowl inside and out with clear acrylic coating. Let it dry, then spray again.

Rainbow Headbands

Rain or shine, make bright headbands and bracelets to match with this sticky trick.

1 Wind the embroidery thread into a small ball, making a ball for each color of thread. Cut the two-sided tape into seven or eight pieces that are each about 2 inches long.

2 Cover the top of the headband with the tape. Peel off the backing from one end piece only. If the tape is wider than the headband, fold it around the headband after you remove the backing.

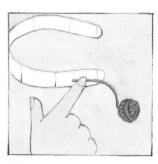

3 Take the end of the thread and press 1 inch onto the sticky tape. This anchor will keep the thread in place when you start wrapping it around the headband.

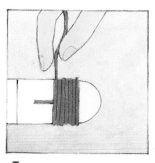

4 Wrap the thread around the headband, starting at the edge of the first piece of tape. Cover the 1-inch anchor piece. As you wrap, each round should be right next to the one before it. Peel off the backing from each piece of tape as you come to it.

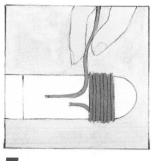

5 To change colors, cut the thread, leaving about a half inch at the end. Press this end onto the tape. Repeat Step 3 to begin a new color. As you wrap, make sure the first color doesn't show through the next color.

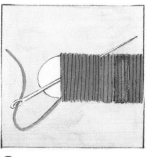

6 To finish, cut the thread. Thread it through the needle and pull it under 10 rounds on the underside of the headband. Snip the thread close to the headband. Dab glue on the underside of both ends of the headband to hold the thread in place.

Use this yarn-wrapping technique to make bracelets, too. You'll need bendable strips of metal called "bracelet blanks," available at craft stores. Cover the bracelet blanks with tape and wrap them up, just like the headbands.

The headband on the right was made with nubby bouclé (boo-CLAY) yarn that you can buy at a fabric shop. To make the belt on this page, put tape on cotton clothesline and wrap it up!

Papier-Mâché Animal

YOU WILL NEED

Time
- 2 hours

Supplies
- 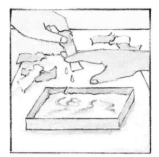 An adult to help you
- Plastic container with cover, 6-cup size
- Measuring cups and measuring spoons
- 4 tablespoons cellulose wallpaper paste
- 4 cups cold water
- Mixing spoon
- An old plastic tablecloth
- Newspapers
- Ruler
- Aluminum foil
- 1-inch-wide masking tape
- Wax paper
- 1-inch-wide sponge brush
- Gesso (a sealer available at art supply stores)
- Acrylic paints
- Paintbrushes (assorted sizes)
- Plastic plate
- Optional: Spackle®, clear acrylic spray coating (follow the directions on the can)

1 Follow Steps 1 and 2 for the papier-mâché bowl on page 10, but tear the newspaper into strips about ½ inch wide by 3 inches long.

2 Squeeze large pieces of foil into an animal shape. Attach pieces like arms or legs with masking tape. Your animal can be from 4 inches to 10 inches tall. Cover the entire animal with pieces of masking tape. Papier-mâché will not stick to foil.

3 Dip a newspaper strip into the wallpaper paste. Run the strip between two fingers to remove extra paste. The strip should be wet, but it should not have globs of paste on it. Lay the strip on your animal. Continue adding pasted strips in an overlapping pattern until the animal is totally covered.

Polka dots, purple spots, pinstripes, too. Make colorful critters for your own zany zoo!

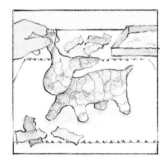

4 Let the animal dry completely on wax paper for a day or so. (Cover the wallpaper paste mixture and store it in a cupboard until you need it again.) Then put a second coat of pasted newspaper strips on the animal. Let the animal dry completely for another day or so.

5 With the sponge brush, paint the animal with gesso. Let it dry for 10 or 15 minutes. If you like, fill any small holes with Spackle. Just press a little into each hole with your fingers.

6 Squeeze paint onto a plastic plate and paint your animal. For the best results, have an adult spray your animal with clear acrylic coating.

Paper Bead Necklace

YOU WILL NEED

Time
- 30-60 minutes

Supplies
- Pencil
- White paper,
  8 ½ by 11 inches
- Ruler
- 2 sheets of shiny,
  good-quality paper
  (see opposite page),
  each 8 ½ by 11 inches
- Scissors
- Wax paper or an old
  plastic tablecloth
- Gloss Mod Podge®
  (a combination of glue
  and finish). You can
  use white glue, too,
  but your beads won't
  be as shiny.
- Small sponge brush
- Juice box straw
- String or dental floss,
  about 32 inches long

1 Trace the triangle pattern on page 46 onto white paper. Cut it out. This will be the pattern for your beads. You can experiment with triangles of different sizes later, but this is a good size to start with.

2 Trace many triangles onto the white side of the shiny paper. Cut them out. Each triangle will make one bead. You will need about 20 beads for a necklace.

3 Cover your work surface with wax paper or an old plastic tablecloth. Lay a paper triangle on your work surface, with the side that you want to show facing up. Brush the Mod Podge onto the triangle.

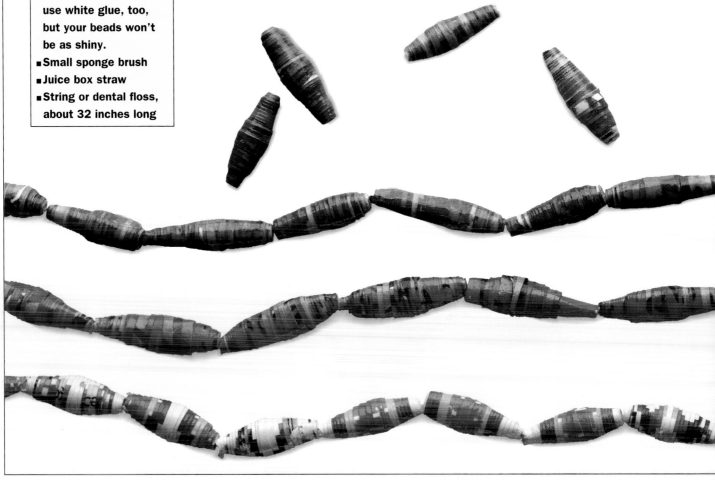

With colorful paper, make beads galore for one necklace, two, or a dozen more!

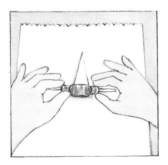

4 Turn over the paper triangle. Roll the wide end of the triangle around the straw, as shown.

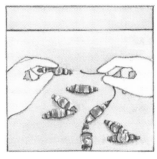

5 Continue rolling until you reach the point of the triangle. Slide the bead off the straw. Make more beads in the same way. **Tip:** When the Mod Podge starts to dry on your hands and the straw, just peel it off or wash it off with warm water.

6 Let the beads dry for about an hour. Then string the beads. Tie the ends of the string or dental floss in a double knot, and you're finished!

Choosing Paper

Gift wrap and covers from magazines and catalogs are perfect for making beads. You might want to experiment with just two or three triangles and beads to be sure you're happy with the colors.

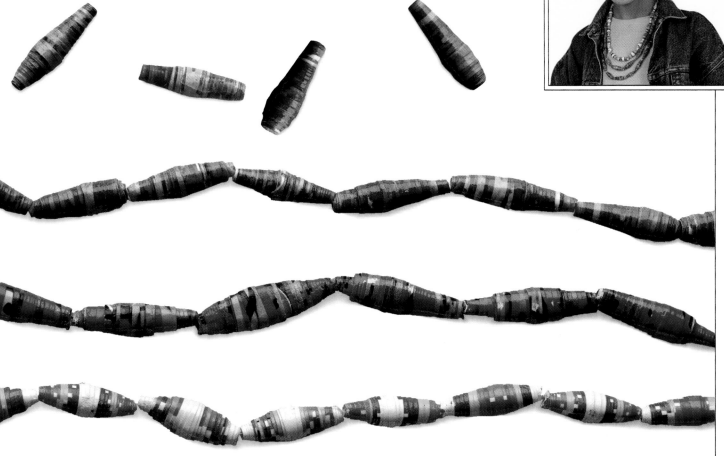

Rose-Colored Glasses

Time
- 45-60 minutes

Supplies
- Pencil
- White paper
- Scissors
- Lightweight cardboard
- Ballpoint pen
- Red cellophane
- Clear tape
- White glue
- Sequins, feathers, glitter, stickers, rhinestones, ribbons

1 Use the pencil to trace the frame and earpiece on page 46 onto white paper. Cut them out to make your own patterns.

2 Place your patterns on the cardboard and trace around them with the pencil. Cut out the frame and two earpieces.

3 Use the ballpoint pen to trace two red cellophane hearts from the pattern on page 46. Cut them out.

Everything's coming up roses! Glamorous glasses add a glow to even the grayest day!

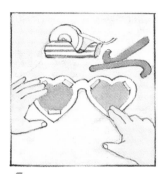

4 Tape the cellophane hearts to the back of the frame (the side with the pencil marks).

5 Cut a small slit on each side of the frame. Insert an earpiece into each slit. Hold the earpieces in place with small pieces of tape on the inside of the frame.

6 Decorate your glasses with sequins, feathers, glitter, stickers, rhinestones, or ribbons.

Fancy Lorgnettes

A lorgnette (lorn YET) is a fancy pair of glasses that has a handle instead of earpieces. Color a pencil or chopstick with a permanent marker or cover it with glue and roll it in glitter. Glue or tape the stick to the back of one side of the frame.

Spring Basket

It's eggs-actly right filled with bright flowers and grass that grows!

Squiggle Eggs

1 Have an adult help you make dye. For each color, mix in a disposable plastic cup
- ½ cup boiling water
- ½ teaspoon (40 drops) of food coloring
- 1 teaspoon white vinegar.

Let the dye cool before using it.

2 Cover the table with newspapers. Then ask an adult to pour about ½ cup of rubber cement into another cup. Tip: Wash your hands with soap before you touch the eggs. If you get grease on an egg, it won't dye evenly.

3 Cut a strip of construction paper about 6 inches long and tape it into a circle. Set an egg on top. Dip a craft stick into the rubber cement and dribble it onto the egg. Let it dry for about 15 minutes. Then turn the egg over and repeat.

4 With a spoon, place the egg into the dye, and you'll start to see your patterns. Leave the egg in the dye until it's the color you want.

5 Remove the egg from the dye with the spoon. Gently pat the egg with a paper towel. Let it dry in the construction paper ring for about 30 minutes.

6 Rub the rubber cement with your fingers. It will come right off, leaving pretty, squiggly designs.

Remember: Don't eat these eggs-tra special eggs! They're just for decoration.

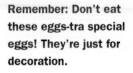

Basket with Real Grass

You will need

Time

- ■ 15 minutes to make,
  7-9 days to grow

Supplies

- ■ A pretty basket
- ■ 2 plastic bags. Put one
  inside the other.
- ■ Vermiculite, available at
  garden centers
- ■ Wheat berries, available at
  health-food stores. Rye-grass
  seed works, too.
- ■ Clear plastic wrap

1 Line the basket with the
plastic bags. Fill the basket
with vermiculite until it's
1 to 2 inches from the top.

2 Spread the wheat berries
thickly on top so they cover
the vermiculite. Add water
until it comes almost to the
top of the vermiculite.

3 Place a layer of plastic
wrap over the basket and put
it in bright, indirect light.

4 When the grass is about an
inch high, remove the plastic
wrap. Put the basket in a
sunny window. You shouldn't
have to water it. In a week or
so, you'll have grass about
6 inches high.

Masterpiece Mugs

YOU WILL NEED

Time
- 30-45 minutes

Supplies
- An adult to help you
- Liquitex® Glossies Acrylic Enamels, sold at craft stores. When a mug is painted with this paint and baked in an oven, the design becomes permanent and dishwasher safe.
- Newspapers
- Ceramic mug
- Plastic plate
- Small paintbrushes
- Damp rag
- Cookie sheet
- Pot holders

1 Read the paint directions. These paints aren't toxic, but don't paint the inside of the mug or anything else that comes in direct contact with food or drinks. Cover your work surface with newspapers.

2 Wash the ceramic mug with dish detergent and water. It must be squeaky clean and dry before you paint. Also, be sure your hands are clean.

3 Shake the paint bottles. Squeeze small blobs of paint on the plate. Paint designs on the outside of the mug with a medium coat of paint. Your strokes shouldn't be too thick or too thin. If you make a mistake, wipe the paint off with a damp rag and try again.

Add a special touch to your gift by pasting your picture on the tag of a tea bag.

22

Turn an ordinary mug into an extraordinary cup of creativity!

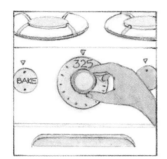

4 Complete your mug by painting your initials and the date on the bottom of the mug. When you're finished painting, clean your brush with water. Let the painted mug dry for at least six hours.

5 Preheat the oven to 325 degrees. Place the painted mug on the cookie sheet. Ask an adult to put the sheet on the middle rack of the oven and bake for 40 minutes. Open a window or turn on the oven fan so the kitchen is well ventilated as the mug bakes.

6 Have an adult use pot holders to remove the cookie sheet from the oven. Let the mug cool completely before you handle it. When it's cool, wrap it up, and present it to someone special!

Pretzel Barrette

Twist up colors you like a lot. Finish them off in a loopy knot!

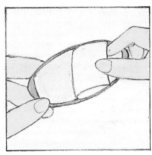

1 Cut a piece of two-sided tape that's just a little shorter than the barrette cover is wide. Press it on top of the barrette cover. Peel off the backing from the tape. If the tape is wider than the barrette, fold it over the barrette top and bottom.

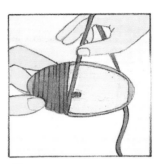

2 Press one inch of the yarn horizontally onto the tape at the end as an anchor. Then wrap the yarn around the barrette cover vertically, going right over the 1-inch piece. Wrap each round close to the one before it, so the barrette cover is hidden.

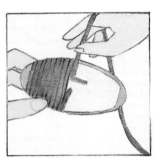

3 To change colors, cut the yarn and press ½ inch of it onto the tape. Begin again with a new color. To finish, cut the yarn to 4 inches long. Thread it through the needle and pull it through the yarn on the underside of the barrette.

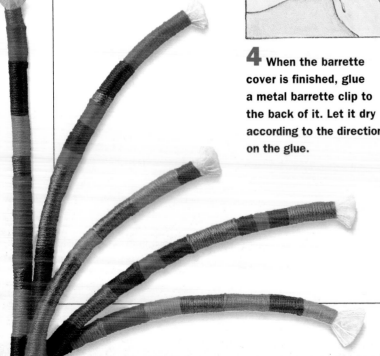

4 When the barrette cover is finished, glue a metal barrette clip to the back of it. Let it dry according to the directions on the glue.

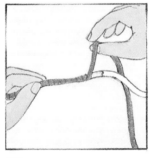

5 To make a pretzel knot, wrap pieces of two-sided tape tightly around the cotton cord. Remove the backing from one piece at a time. Then wrap the yarn around the cord, just as you did around the barrette.

6 Tie the rope into a pretzel knot (see opposite page). Using a cotton swab, put glue on the back of the pretzel knot and press the knot onto the barrette. Color the ends of the barrette with a permanent marker.

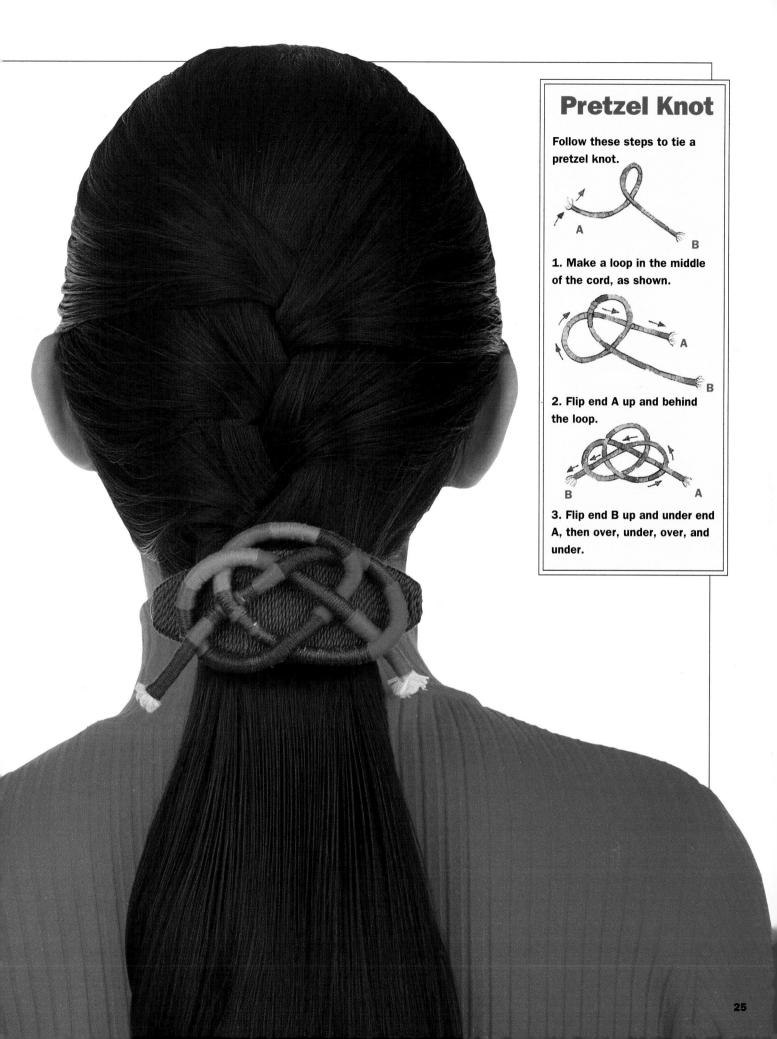

Pretzel Knot

Follow these steps to tie a pretzel knot.

A

B

1. Make a loop in the middle of the cord, as shown.

A

B

2. Flip end A up and behind the loop.

B

A

3. Flip end B up and under end A, then over, under, over, and under.

Star Candle Holders

1 Use the pencil to trace the star pattern on page 46 onto the white paper. Cut it out. Now trace your paper star onto the cardboard. Cut out the cardboard star and the hole in the middle of the star.

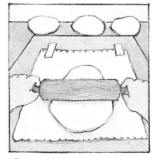

2 Divide the Sculpey into six equal pieces so it will be easier to work with. Knead each piece for one minute. Tape a piece of wax paper to the cutting board. Then roll out a piece of Sculpey to a ¼-inch thickness with the rolling pin.

3 Put the cardboard star on top of the rolled-out Sculpey. Use the small knife to cut around the outside edge of the cardboard star. Cut out the hole in the center, too. Do the same to make more stars.

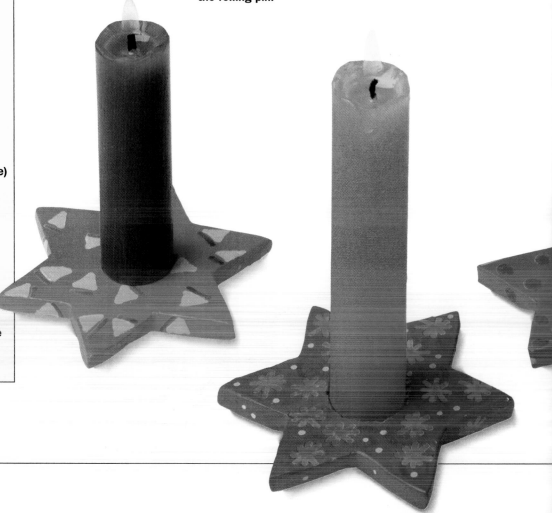

Starlight, star bright!
Make candles sparkle for a special night!

4 Bake the stars in the oven in a glass baking dish, carefully following the directions on the Sculpey box. Have an adult remove them when they're done. Let them cool thoroughly.

5 Cover your work surface with wax paper. Ask an adult to help you glue the tapered end of a doll pin stand to the bottom of each star. Follow the instructions on the glue container. Let the glue dry thoroughly.

6 Paint the undersides of the candle holders first. Let the paint dry, and then turn over the stars and paint the tops. Acrylic paint dries in 1 to 2 hours. If necessary, ask an adult to shave the ends of the candles so they fit in the holders. Then ask the adult to help you light your starry candles!

Fancy Frames

With tissue paper or gift wrap, create a fabulous photo finish.

1 Cut designs from the wrapping paper, making sure the designs will fit on the front of the framing mat. Set these aside until Step 6. Then rip the tissue paper into pieces, each about 2 inches wide and 2 inches long.

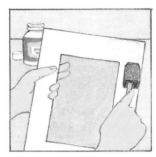

2 Cover the table with wax paper or an old plastic tablecloth. Hold the mat in your hand. Use the brush to apply Mod Podge lightly to the front, sides, and back edges of the mat. Hold the mat gently, so it doesn't bend.

3 Put a piece of tissue paper onto the wet Mod Podge, wrapping the tissue paper around the edge of the mat. Lightly brush more Mod Podge on top of the tissue paper to hold it in place.

4 Put another piece of tissue paper onto the mat, overlapping the new piece onto the first piece. Lightly brush Mod Podge on top of this new piece. Keep adding Mod Podge and tissue paper to the mat in this way until the whole front of the mat is covered.

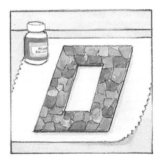

5 Lay the mat flat on the wax paper to dry thoroughly. This will take about an hour. While the mat is drying, clean the paintbrush by rinsing it in water.

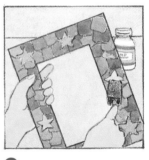

6 To add the designs you cut in Step 1, dab Mod Podge onto the mat, lay the designs on it, and brush Mod Podge on top. Tip: Don't go over the designs too many times with Mod Podge or the color from the tissue paper will smear. Let the mat dry.

Put the finished mat and your favorite photo into a store-bought picture frame like the one shown above.

You can make your own frame from foam core, sold at craft stores. Have an adult cut the foam core frame. Decorate it and tape a snapshot to the back. Use poster putty to hang the frame on a wall.

Rubber Band Stamps

With your imaginative stamp, all your mail will be a special delivery!

YOU WILL NEED

Time
- 30-60 minutes

Supplies
- Small blocks of wood from 1 to 3 inches across. They can be squares, rectangles, or any other shape.
- Two-sided tape with peel-off backing
- Scissors
- Rubber bands of various widths
- Stamp pads with washable ink, or washable markers
- Scrap paper
- Plain stationery, envelopes, note cards
- Paper towels

1 Cover one side of a wooden block with two-sided tape. You may need more than one piece of tape to cover it. Trim off any pieces of tape that hang over the edges of the block. Don't remove the peel-off backing from the tape yet.

2 Cut several rubber bands of the same type into pieces of different sizes. Arrange the pieces until you have a design you like. Tip: Use only one kind of rubber band on each block. Don't overlap pieces of rubber band. See the tip for making letters on the opposite page.

3 When your design is ready, remove the peel-off backing from the tape. Piece by piece, put your rubber-band design onto the sticky tape. Trim off any pieces of rubber band that hang over the edge of the block.

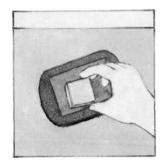

4 Now you're ready to use your stamp. Press your stamp on an ink pad a few times. You can also apply color to the stamp with a marker. Be sure you get an even coating of color onto the stamp.

5 Press the stamp firmly and evenly onto the paper. Tip: Putting a magazine under your paper will give you a better print. Practice on scrap paper a few times before you stamp on good paper.

6 To use the same stamp with different colors, clean the stamp by pressing it a few times onto a damp paper towel. Then press it onto a dry paper towel. The stamp should be dry before you try a second color.

July

Dear Aunt Lisa,
Thank you for my photo album. I've filled half of it with pictures from my birthday party! There's a great pict. of you u.

A Paper Doll of You

With a wardrobe of the most wonderful outfits you ever dreamed of—or dreamed up!

YOU WILL NEED

Time
- 45-60 minutes

Supplies
- An adult to help you
- 35-mm camera and color film
- Bathing suit or leotard
- X-acto® knife
- Foam core, 12 inches by 18 inches or larger
- Ruler
- Rubber cement. Be sure to read the directions and warning labels on the container.
- Paper—colored paper, gift wrap, metallic paper, wallpaper, even aluminum foil. (Ask for free discontinued sample wallpaper books at a wallpaper store.)
- Pencil
- Scissors
- Optional: Glue stick or white glue
- Optional trimmings: Lace doilies, sequins, glitter, and feathers to decorate the clothes

1 Ask an adult to take a few pictures of you dressed in a bathing suit or leotard. Stand in front of a light-colored wall, and hold out your arms slightly from your body. Have a photo shop blow up the photo you like best so that your doll is a little less than 18 inches.

2 Ask an adult to use the X-acto knife to cut a strip 1¼ by 18 inches off the long edge of the foam core. Fold this strip in half. This will be the base that lets the paper doll stand up.

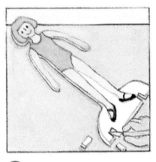

3 Ask an adult to rubber cement the photo to the large piece of foam core, following the directions on the container. Then have the adult cut out the doll with an X-acto knife. Ask the adult to leave a stand around the feet and to cut out two slots in the stand.

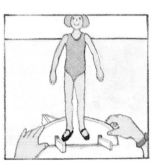

4 Stand up the doll by inserting the folded strip of foam core from Step 2 into the slots.

5 Place your doll face down on the wrong side of the paper. Lightly trace her outline with a pencil. Lift her up, and then draw an outfit around the outline of the doll. Add tabs at the shoulders and wherever they are needed to hold the clothes onto the doll.

6 Cut out the outfit. Decorate it by gluing on optional trimmings.

Fabric Clothing

You can make fabric clothing from material that doesn't fray. Use felt, for example, to make a cheerleader or skating outfit. To fasten the felt clothes to your doll, put Velcro® dots on your doll and each outfit.

Collection Necklace

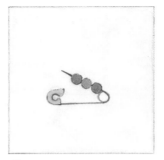

1 The basic necklace pattern is safety pin, snap swivel, safety pin, snap swivel, and so on. Start with a safety pin. Open it and put beads or a charm on it. Close the safety pin.

2 Open the hook on a snap swivel. Hang a bead or a charm on it. Put the hook through the head of the pin. Close the hook.

3 Open a second safety pin. Put the point of the pin through the circle loop on the end of the snap swivel. Put beads or a charm on the pin. Close the pin.

Turn trinkets into treasure with this sparkly necklace of everyday gems.

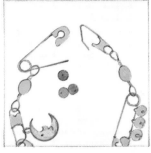

4 Continue until the necklace is the length you want. Then attach the last snap swivel to the safety pin you started with. You may first have to remove the charm or beads you put on that safety pin. Replace them after you attach the snap swivel.

Necklace Extras

You can add to your necklace any gold, silver, or brightly colored items that fit on the pin or snap swivel or that have a hook for hanging.

Jewelry box: Charms, baby rings or lockets, single earrings, perfect attendance bars or pins

Workshop or garage: Washers, nuts, eye screws

Craft store: Bells, beads, shells

Make your own beads from Fimo or Sculpey clay, too. Be sure they are skinny enough to fit on the closed pin or snap.

Pretty Paperweights

Don't "weight" another minute. Polish hot rocks into cool keepsakes—now!

YOU WILL NEED

Time
- 2 hours baking, 10-20 minutes making

Supplies
-  An adult to help you
- Smooth stones or rocks, about the size of a paperweight
- Damp rag or brush
- Cookie sheet covered with aluminum foil
- Pot holders
- Newspapers
- Old, broken crayons– try gold and silver
- A soft rag

1 If the rocks are dirty, clean them with a brush or damp rag. Let them dry. Place them on a cookie sheet covered with aluminum foil.

2 With an adult's help, put the cookie sheet into an oven set at 200 degrees. Let the stones "bake" for 2 hours. While you wait, cover the table with a thick layer of newspapers.

3 After 2 hours, ask an adult to take the cookie sheet out of the oven. Using a pot holder, place the rocks onto the newspaper. Always use a pot holder when touching the rocks.

4 To make designs, press down with the crayons on the tops of the hot rocks right away, letting the wax melt. To draw pictures, like flowers or fish, let the rocks cool for about 5 minutes before you draw on them.

5 Put the finished rocks back on the cookie sheet. Let them cool overnight.

6 The next day, polish each rock with a soft rag until it looks shiny. This will take a minute or two.

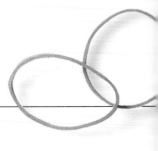

Fish Headdress

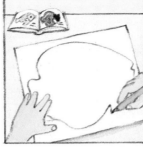

1 Look through a book on fish for ideas about which type of fish you'd like to be. Use the pencil to draw an outline of the whole fish on a piece of poster board. Make your fish as large as possible.

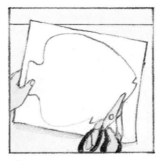

2 Cut out the fish. Trace around this fish on the second piece of poster board, and cut out the second fish.

3 Cover the table with newspapers. Paint or color the two outsides of your fish. Let it dry. It doesn't have to look exactly like a real fish. Just use your imagination and have fun!

Become an imaginary creature of the deep in this fantastical Halloween headdress.

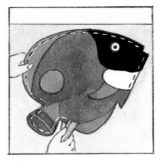

4 Staple the outer edges of the two sides together all the way around, except for the bottom, where your head goes.

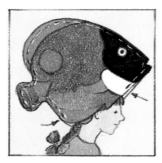

5 Put on the headdress and ask a helper to pinch the bottom of the fish together in front of your forehead and behind your head.

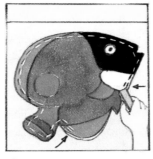

6 Staple the fish together in these two spots so the headdress fits snugly. Staple a few times to hold the headdress securely.

Try making other giant headdresses of flowers or animals.

Paste-Paint Recipe

Make your own bright, bold paint to decorate a rainbow of gifts for family and friends.

1 Put 4 cups of cold water in the saucepan. Whisk in 8 level tablespoons of cornstarch.

2 Working with an adult, cook the mixture on the stove over medium heat, stirring constantly. When the mixture is bubbly and thick, remove the pan from the heat and let it cool for about 30 minutes.

3 While the paste is still slightly warm, place the sieve over the bowl. Pour the paste through the sieve to remove any lumps.

4 When the paste is completely cool, whisk it with quick, hard strokes until it is smooth. It should look like thin pudding. If it's much too thick, whisk in a little water—a tablespoon at a time.
Note: If you're not making your paint right away, you can refrigerate the cornstarch mix in a covered container for one to two weeks.

5 To make the paste-paint, the cornstarch mixture must be at room temperature. Put 2 tablespoons of cornstarch paste into a plastic cup. Add 1 tablespoon of acrylic paint to the paste. Mix well with a craft stick or plastic spoon. If you want a darker color, add more paint.

6 Make other colors in the same way. Cover the cups tightly with plastic wrap when not in use and store them in a cupboard. The paste-paint will last for a week or two.

Patterns to Practice

Paint freckles and speckles, squiggles and stripes, zapples and dapples, and zigzag delights!

Combs

YOU WILL NEED

Time
- 10 or 15 minutes for painting practice

Supplies
- Pencil
- Cardboard
- Scissors
- Ruler
- 2-inch sponge brush
- Paste-paint
- Paper or cardboard to practice on

1 Draw a comb on the cardboard. Cut it out. You can make different combs to get different designs. They can be from 1 inch across to 3 inches across.

2 Use the sponge brush to apply paste-paint to paper or lightweight cardboard. Then pull the combs through it, making interesting designs. Rinse out the sponge brush when you're through, so you can use it again.

Sponges

YOU WILL NEED

Time
- 10 or 15 minutes for painting practice

Supplies
- Sea sponge big enough to fit in the palm of your hand
- Water
- Paste-paint
- Paper or cardboard to practice on

1 Dip a damp sea sponge into the paste-paint. Dab it a few times on a piece of scrap paper to remove extra paint. Then dab it lightly all over the surface you're painting.

2 When you're finished, rinse out the sea sponge so you can use it again.

Pots and Boxes

With a splash of paint, give ordinary boxes and flowerpots colorful pizzazz!

1 Cover your work surface with wax paper or an old plastic tablecloth. Put on the disposable gloves. With an adult, carefully read the directions on the BIN can.

2 Working with an adult, paint one coat of BIN onto your flowerpot or wooden box. Let it sit for about 30 minutes until it is totally dry. Then apply a second coat and let it dry.

3 If you're designing with a cardboard comb, use a sponge brush to paint a coat of paste-paint onto the pot or box. Before the paste-paint dries, pull the comb through it to create interesting patterns.
Tip: If you make a mistake, just paint over it with the sponge brush and start again!

4 If you're designing with a sponge, use a damp sea sponge to apply paste-paint to the flowerpot or wooden box.

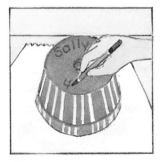

5 Let the pot or box dry. Write your name and date on the bottom.

6 To protect the finished pot or box, you can ask an adult to spray it with clear acrylic spray, following the directions on the can.

Fill the painted flowerpot
with a pretty plant!

VIP Portfolio

A Very Important Project for a Very Important Person—you!

1 Cover your work surface with newspaper or an old plastic tablecloth. Place the heavy paper on top and paste-paint it following the directions on page 41 for comb or sponge patterns. If you're using combs, be sure to work quickly. If the paint sinks into the paper, you won't see the patterns. Let the paper dry.

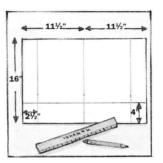

2 Put the painted side of the paper facing down on your work surface. Draw a light pencil line down the middle of the paper. Draw two more vertical lines 2½ inches in from each side. Then draw a horizontal line 4 inches up from the bottom.

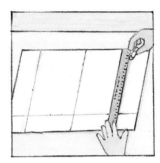

3 Crease the penciled lines so they will fold more easily. To do this, hold a ruler on the fold line and run a large paper clip down the ruler, pressing hard into the paper.

4 Fold the paper in, as shown. Round off the top corners with scissors.

5 Tie a knot on the end of each ribbon. Make a small hole inside each side crease and pull the ribbons through. Refold the portfolio sides. Then fold the bottom up and use the tape to fasten it to the sides.

6 Close the portfolio and tie the ribbons into a bow to hold it together. If it's a gift, write a special message to put inside.

Decorate wrapping paper and framing mats with paste-paint. Make gift tags and ornaments, too.

Patterns

Trace these patterns, following the directions for each craft.

Rose-Colored Glasses, page 18

Paper Bead Necklace, page 16

Star Candle Holders   page 26